Long Walks and Intimate Talks

Stories and Poems by Grace Paley
Paintings by Vera B. Williams

WOMEN AND PEACE SERIES
The Feminist Press
at The City University of New York
New York

Published 1991 by The Feminist Press at The City University of
New York, 311 East 94 Street, New York, NY 10128

Distributed by The Talman Company, 150 Fifth Avenue, New York,
NY 10011

95 94 93 92 91 6 5 4 3 2 1

"On the Subway Station," "The Street," and "People in My Family"
reprinted by permission of Tilbury House, Publishers, from *Leaning
Forward* by Grace Paley, 1985.

Library of Congress Cataloging-in-Publication Data

Paley, Grace.
   Long walks and intimate talks / poems and stories by Grace Paley ;
paintings by Vera Williams.
      p.   cm.
   ISBN 1-55861-043-X (cloth) : $29.95. — ISBN 1-55861-044-8 (paper) :
$12.95
   1. Peace—Literary collections.   I. Williams, Vera B.   II. Title.
PS3566.A46L66   1991
813'.54—dc20   90-27844
                                                              CIP

This publication is made possible, in part, by public funds from the
New York State Council on the Arts and the National Endowment for
the Arts. This volume was inspired by the date book titled *365 Reasons
Not to Have Another War*, published by the War Resisters League and
New Society Publishers. The Feminist Press is grateful to these orga-
nizations for their cooperation on this project.

Interior design by Vera B. Williams and Barbara Hirshkowitz
Cover design by Vera B. Williams and Paula Martinac

Printed in the United States of America

For Fay I wish
we'd talked more

Grace
Paley

Flight
of the

Mind

July '93

Introduction

Vera and I come from the same neighborhood in the Bronx, separated by two elevated subways (a linguistic trick, but a fact). We have worked together in and out of the War Resisters League, Women's Pentagon Action, women's affinity groups, mobilization, Central American actions. We have sat down together in front of federal buildings, Wall Street brokerage offices, traffic in Washington, scary but careful horses.

Surprising—to ourselves too—we are not old friends. I had heard of her and never have forgotten her *Liberation* magazine cover designs—the Vietnamese child's head that rolled across our consciences, a marble of pain.

When she asked me to work with her on this book I said, "OK, Why Not?" About a week later I said, "Absolutely, yes." There were poems and prose pieces I'd put off for a long time. Vera had told me she'd been longing to paint a series of faces out of imagination and remembrance. Of course I knew the books she'd illustrated and written, physically beautiful books with a kind of deep politics, meaning the daily life of black white brown children in the grown-up world. This was the right moment and the right person to think with.

So we worked that year, sometimes together, more often alone. We thought this would be OK because of all our walks and rallies and arrests. Our minds, having taken hold in the Bronx of the thirties and forties, were on the same things.

We hoped that our work would, by its happiness and sadness, demonstrate against militarists, racists, earth poisoners, women haters, all those destroyers of days. One common purpose would be to celebrate the day, which is its own reason for peace, to praise and offer to its inherent beauty and reality our work as daily movement people and artists.

And of course we're pleased to reappear with new drawings, poems, and prose pieces. We're proud that our book is one among all the works of all those women artists, storytellers, historians, some of whom lived long ago and far away, and some of whom are our own neighborhood sisters who The Feminist Press has published into a world that had forgotten them, or never knew them.

And now it does.

Grace Paley

Midrash on Happiness

What she meant by happiness, she said, was the following: she meant having (or having had) (or continuing to have) everything. By everything, she meant, first, the children, then a dear person to live with, preferably a man, but not necessarily, (by live with, she meant for a long time but not necessarily). Along with and not in preferential order, she required three or four best women friends to whom she could tell every personal fact and then discuss on the widest deepest and most hopeless level, the economy, the constant, unbeatable, cruel war economy, the slavery of the American worker to the idea of that economy, the complicity of male people in the whole structure, the dumbness of men (including her preferred man) on this subject. By dumbness, she meant everything dumbness has always meant: silence and stupidity. By silence she meant refusal to speak; by stupidity she meant refusal to hear. For happiness she required women to walk with. To walk in the city arm in arm with a woman friend (as her mother had with aunts and cousins so many years ago) was just plain essential. Oh! those long walks and intimate talks, better than standing alone on the most admirable mountain or in the handsomest forest or hay-blown field (all of which were certainly splendid occupations for the wind-starved soul). More important even (though maybe less sweet because of age) than the old walks with boys she'd walked with as a girl, that nice bunch of worried left-wing boys who flew (always slightly handicapped by that idealistic wing) into a dream of paid-up mortgages with a small room for opinion and solitude in the corner of home. Oh do you remember those fellows, Ruthy?

Remember? Well, I'm married to one.

But she had, Faith continued, democratically tried walking in the beloved city with a man, but the effort had failed since from about that age—twenty-seven or eight—he had felt an obligation, if a young woman passed, to turn abstractedly away, in the middle of the most personal conversation or even to say confidentially, wasn't she something?—or clasping his plaid shirt, at the heart's level, oh my god! The purpose of this: perhaps to work a nice quiet appreciation into thunderous heartbeat as he had been taught on pain of sexual death. For happiness, she also required work to do in this world and bread on the table. By work to do she included the important work of

raising children righteously up. By righteously she meant that along with being useful and speaking truth to the community, they must do no harm. By harm she meant not only personal injury to the friend the lover the coworker the parent (the city the nation) but also the stranger; she meant particularly the stranger in all her or his difference, who, because we were strangers in Egypt, deserves special goodness for life or at least until the end of strangeness. By bread on the table, she meant no metaphor but truly bread as her father had ended every single meal with a hunk of bread. By hunk, she was describing one of the attributes of good bread.

Suddenly she felt she had left out a couple of things: Love. Oh yes, she said, for she was talking, talking all this time, to patient Ruth and they were walking for some reason in a neighborhood where she didn't know the children, the pizza places or the vegetable markets. It was early evening and she could see lovers walking along Riverside Park with their arms around one another, turning away from the sun which now sets among the new apartment houses of New Jersey, to kiss. Oh I forgot, she said, now that I notice, Ruthy I think I would die without love. By love she probably meant she would die without being *in* love. By *in* love she meant the acuteness of the heart at the sudden sight of a particular person or the way over a couple of years of interested friendship one is suddenly stunned by the lungs' longing for more and more breath in the presence of that friend, or nearly drowned to the knees by the salty spring that seems to beat for years on our vaginal shores. Not to omit all sorts of imaginings which assure great spiritual energy for months and when luck follows truth, years.

Oh sure, love. I think so too, sometimes, said Ruth, willing to hear Faith out since she had been watching the kissers too, but I'm really not so sure. Nowadays it seems like pride, I mean overweening pride, when you look at the children and think we don't have time to do much (by time Ruth meant both her personal time and the planet's time). When I read the papers and hear all this boom boom bellicosity, the guys out-daring each other, I see we have to change it all—the world—without killing it absolutely—without killing it, that'll be the trick the kids'll have to figure out. Until that begins, I don't understand happiness—what you mean by it.

Then Faith was ashamed to have wanted so much and so little all at the same time—to be so easily and personally satisfied in this terrible place, when everywhere vast public suffering rose in reeling waves from the round earth's nation-states—hung in the satellite-watched air and settled in no time at all into TV sets and newsrooms. It was all there. Look up and the news of halfway round the planet is falling on us all. So for all these conscientious and technical reasons, Faith was ashamed. It was clear that happiness could not be worthwhile, with so much conversation and so little revolutionary change. Of course, Faith said, I know all that. I do, but sometimes walking with a friend I forget the world.

Families

The sheep families are out in the meadow
Caddy and her two big lambs Gruff and Veronica
Veronica raises her curly head then bends to the grass
Usefully she shits   green grass and wool is her work

Gruff is going away   he will become something else
Father of generations?   What?   more likely meat that
is a male in war or pasture   his work is meat

I Gave Away That Kid

I gave away that kidlike he was an old button
    Here old button get off of me
    I don't need you anymore
    go on get out of here
    get into the army
    sew yourself onto the colonel's shirt
    or the captain's fly   jackass
    don't you have any sense
    don't you read the papers
    why are you leaving now?

That kid walked out of here like he was the cat's pyjamas
    what are you wearing p j's for   you damn fool?
    why are you crying   you couldn't
    get another job anywhere anyways
    go march to the army's drummer
    be a man like all your dead uncles
    then think of something else to do

Lost him, sorry about that the president said
    he was a good boy
    never see one like him again
    Why don't you repeat that your honor
    why don't you sizzle up the meaning
    of that sentence for your breakfast
    why don't you stick him in a prayer
and count to ten before my wife gets you.

That boy is a puddle in Beirut   the paper says
    scraped up for singing in church
    too bad   too bad is a terrible tune
    it's no song at all   how come you sing it?

I gave away that kidlike he was an old button
    Here old button get off ame
    I don't need you anymore
    go on get out of here
    get into the army
    sew yourself onto the colonel's shirt
    or the captain's fly   jackass
    don't you have any sense
    don't you read the papers
    why are you leaving now?

In San Salvador I

Come   look   they said
here are the photograph albums
these are our children

We are called The Mothers of the Disappeared
we are also the mothers of those who were seen once more
and then photographed   sometimes parts of them
could not be found

a breast   an eye   an arm is missing
sometimes a whole stomach
that is why we are called   The Mothers
of the Disappeared   although we have these large
heavy photograph albums full of beautiful
torn faces

In San Salvador II

The one woman spoke   About my son
she said   I want to tell you   This
is what happened

                I heard a cry   Mother
mother   keep the door closed   a scream
the high voice of my son   his scream
jumped into my belly   his voice
boiled there and boiled until hot water
ran down my thigh

                The following week I waited
by the fire making tortilla   I heard What?
the voice of my second son   Mother quickly
turn your back to the door   turn your back
to the window

                And one day of the third week
my third son called me   oh mother please
hurry up   hold out your apron   they are
stealing my eyes

                And then in the fourth week   my
fourth son   No

    No   It was morning   he stood
in the doorway   he was taken right
there   before my eyes the parts of
the body of my son were tormented   are
you listening?   do you understand
this story?   there was only one
child   one boy   like Mary   I had
only one son

Conversations

My husband's mother lived in Florida on the sandy shore of a small lake in the middle of an orange grove that looked something like a child's painting, based in the color of sand with an occasional spear of green green grass bending this way and that. She was dying and wanted to ask a couple of questions about life. We could speak to her only at lunch—briefly—and later at supper. She didn't eat much but it was the hour of her little strength and she offered it to us.

One evening at supper she asked me about Women's Lib. She and her best friend (also very sick) had been talking about it. She said she thought I might know something about it. What was it like? Did it mean there would be women lawyers?

Yes.

Would they work for women?

Oh surely, I said.

Would women get paid the same? Was that the idea?

One of them, I answered. Equal pay at least.

Would women be free of men bossing them around?

Hopefully, I said. Though it might take the longest amount of time since it would involve lots of changes in men.

Oh they won't like that a bit, she said. Would people love their daughters then as much as their sons?

Maybe more, I said.

Not fair again, she said slyly.

But that wasn't all, I said. Most of the Womens Libbers I knew really didn't want to have a piece of the men's pie. They thought that pie was kind of poisonous, toxic, reallyfull of weapons, poison gases, all kinds of mean junk we didn't even want a slice of.

She was tired. That's a lot she said. Then she went upstairs to sleep.

In the morning she surprised us. She came down for breakfast. I couldn't sleep she said. I was up all night thinking of what you said. You know she said, there isn't a thing I've done in my life that I haven't done for some man. Dress up or go out or take a job or quit it or go home or leave. Or even be quiet or say something nice, things like that. You know I was up all night thinking about you and especially those young women. I couldn't stop thinking about what wonderful lives they're going to have.

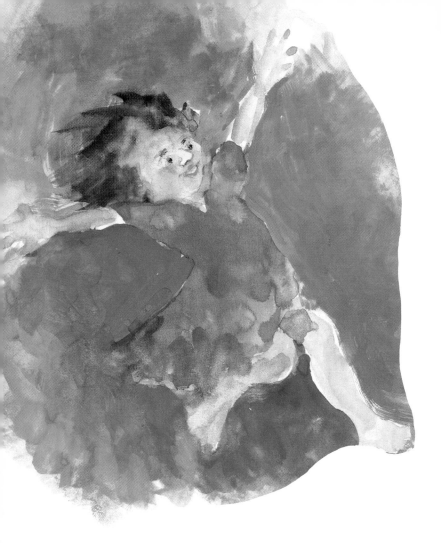

The Five Day Week

The five-day week was set like a firecracker
The five-day week   ah   like a long bath in the
                first bathtub of God
The five-day week was sunny all year   (I remember)
The five-day week gave at last what she'd always longed for
                a cheerful noisy companion
                to Sabbath calm Queen of days

The Street

The boys from St. Bernard's
and the boys from
Our Lady of Pompeii
converge on the corner of Bleecker and Bank

There is a grinding of snowballs
and a creaking of ice

The name of our Lord is invoked

But for such healthy tough warriors
He has other deaths in mind

Sulky
They part

On the Subway Station

The child is speaking to the father
he is looking into the father's eyes
father doesn't answer
child is speaking Vietnamese
father doesn't answer
child is speaking English
father doesn't answer
The father is staring at a mosaic in blue and green
and lavender three small ships in harbor
set again and again in the white tiled
beautiful   old   unrenovated subway
station   Clark Street   Brooklyn

One Morning at Edie's

One Saturday morning when Faith came to visit Edie, there were five little girls sitting around the kitchen table. There was a soup plate full of crayons and a stack of yellow school paper.

On one kitchen wall some Aztecs dressed in red and gold were mounting a ziggurat. At the pinnacle one fierce male heart was being cut out with a curved sword by a kingly looking person. Down the high steps, about thirty heart-shaped hearts had been flung.

That's some tough mural, Faith said.

A heart doesn't really look like a heart, said Tessa, the tallest, maybe oldest, little girl.

Well he was a furious kid, Edie said. I bet that picture's about eight years old. I bet you won't believe me. The children and Faith all shouted, We believe you, we believe you. All right, OK, enough. Well he came to see me here at home a few days ago. Did I really draw stuff like that? he asked. Then he takes a pen and signs this wild bloody drawing, Peter Drummon, Dreamer Peacemaker. Then he can't stop so—well—you can see, Lifetime Fighter Against War and Racism—he almost quit but remembered Sexism. Give me the pen, I said.

You shouldn't have stopped him, Faith said. We might've learned what comes next.

He must be crazy that boy. Anyway I hate that picture, Luisa said.

Not me, I love it, Elena said.

I love *that* one—over the sink see—the Indian man is bringing corn to the white man? That's so kind.

Why he wears that hat, the white man. Loco, said Luisa.

She's my cousin. She's only in first grade, Tessa said.

The girls speak English most of the time, Edie explained, but when they're excited with one another they run into Spanish, a Puerto Rican Spanish that throws out most s's and eludes at high speed Edie's two-year course in Spanish for teachers. Every now and then they decide it's time to help Edie. Elena will take her hand and lead her around the kitchen. El frig a dor. Repité. Edie says friga dor. Bueno. That's often enough for one day.

What are you drawing? Faith asked Sandra. El agua. Los politos. Sandra felt like a strict teacher. Entiende?

I wish I'd gone into teaching, Faith said. Instead of these stupid jobs. I don't even know what to call them.

Office jobs, Edie said. You haven't done too bad. Kept the boys in potato chips.

No, no. I never did what I wanted to do.

What did you want to do, asked Sandra, be a boss?

Well, something else.

Don't give up the ship, Tessa said.

No, no. I'm OK really Tessa.

You married? You got a man?

Well, yes and no.

Keep your money in a drawer or a pillow or something.

Really? Faith smiled. She had always done that.

She didn't get married. Elena pointed to Edie. Now she's too old.

There's old men, Sandra suggested.

No, no. If they're too old. Ugh.

But nobody bosses her, Tessa said, hugging Edie's arm protectively. She lets us come over all the time. Right?

Oh you kids. That's it. You're bigger bosses than anyone. Put away the crayons. OK, I want to go take a nice walk with my pal.

They all begged to make one more drawing. For you teacher dear. For your friend.

As usual Edie said OK. One more. Then that's it.

And don't you worry, you friend, you might make boss some day. My grandma, abuelita abualita, Sandra said as though reminding herself, then louder, my grandma says you be good you be all right. Jesus will take care of you.

Oh, said Faith, I get it. She kissed Sandra's soft little cheek. From now on, I'll be good.

For Danny

My son enters the classroom
There are thirty two children waiting for him
He dreams that he will teach them to read
His head is full of the letters that words are looking for

Because of his nature
his fingers are flowers
Here is a rose   he says   look   it grew right
into the letter R

They like that idea very much   they lean forward
So he says   now spell garden
They write it correctly in their notebooks   maybe
          because the word rose is in it

My son is happy
Now spell sky
For this simple word the children
turn their eyes down and away   doesn't he know
the city has been quarreling with the sky all of their lives

Well, he says spell   home   he's a little frightened
          to ask this of them   What?
They laugh   they can't hear him say
What's so funny?   they jump
up out of their seats laughing

My son says hopefully   it's three o'clock
but they don't want to leave   where will they go?
they want to stay right here in the classroom   they probably
want to spell garden again   they want
to examine his hand

It is the responsibility

It is the responsibility of society to let the poet be a poet
It is the responsibility of the poet to be a woman
It is the responsibility of the poet to stand on street corners
        giving out poems and beautifully written leaflets
        also leaflets they can hardly bear to look at
        because of the screaming rhetoric
It is the responsibility of the poet to be lazy to hang out and
        prophecy
It is the responsibility of the poet not to pay war taxes
It is the responsibility of the poet to go in and out of ivory
        towers and two-room apartments on Avenue C
        and buckwheat fields and army camps
It is the responsibility of the male poet to be a woman
It is the responsibility of the female poet to be a woman
It is the poet's responsibility to speak truth to power as the
        Quakers say
It is the poet's responsibility to learn the truth from the
        powerless
It is the responsibility of the poet to say many times: there is no
        freedom without justice and this means economic
        justice and love justice
It is the responsibility of the poet to sing this in all the original
        and traditional tunes of singing and telling poems
It is the responsibility of the poet to listen to gossip and pass it
        on in the way story tellers decant the story of life
There is no freedom without fear and bravery. There is no
        freedom unless
        earth and air and water continue and children
        also continue
It is the responsibility of the poet to be a woman to keep an eye on
        this world and cry out like Cassandra, but be
        listened to this time.

Spoken in almost exactly these words at the American Poetry Review Conference on Poetry and the Writer's Responsibility to Society, Spring 1984.

In Aix

The doves   the speckled doves
are cooing in French   in high
female French   the shutters
clatter against their latches

The rain is the rain of Aix a-
wash in old paintings of
marsh and mist by Granet the rain
splashes the shutters the rain is

bathed in the clouds of Chernobyl
last night on the evening
news we heard how nightingales
blowing north from Poland
folded their wings   fell over
the border and died in Germany

Cop Tales

At the Wall Street Action in October 1979, the police were on one side of the sawhorses. We were on the other. We were blocking Wall Street workers. The police were blocking us. One of them was very interested in solar housing. Our solar expert explained the science and economics of it all. Another cop from Long Island worried a lot about Shoreham. "Can't do anything about it," he said. "They'll build it. I hate it. I live there. What am I going to do?"

That could be a key to the police I thought. They have no hope. Cynical. They're mad at us because we have a little hope in the midst of our informed worries.

Then he said, looking at the Bread and Puppet Theater's stilt dancers, "Look at that, what's going on here? People running around the street dancing. They're going every which way. It ain't organized." We started to tell him how important the dancers were. "No, no, that's okay" he said. "The anti-war demonstrations were like this at first, mixed up, but they got themselves together. You'll get yourself together too. In a couple of years you'll know how to do it better."

Earlier, about 6 a.m., two cops wearing blue hardhats passed. One of them looked behind him. "Here come the horses," he said. "Let's get the hell out of here!" And they moved at top casual walking speed in the opposite direction.

Also at 6 a.m., but about fifteen years ago, we would walk up and down before the Whitehall Street Induction Center wearing signs that said "I Support Draft Refusal." It wouldn't take more than a couple of hours for the system to gather up its young victims, stuff them into wagons, and start them off on their terrible journey. At 9:30 on one of those mornings, about twenty women sat down all across the street to prevent the death wagons from moving. They sat for about thirty minutes. Then a plainclothesman approached an older gray-haired woman, "Missus, you don't want to get arrested." "I have to," she said. "My grandson's in Vietnam." Gently they removed her. Then with billy clubs, a dozen uniformed men moved up and down that line of young women, dragging them away, by their arms, their hair, beating them, I remember, (and Norma Becker remembers) mostly in the breast.

Last May at the rainy Armed Forces Day Parade, attended by officers, their wives, and Us, some of Us were arrested by a couple of Cops for Christ. At the desk, as they took our names, smiling, they gave us "Cops for Christ" leaflets. We gave "Disarm for Human Life" leaflets.

Another year, one of the first really large antidraft actions—also at the Induction Center at dawn. We were to surround the building. The famous people, or *Notables* as the Vietnamese used to say, sat down to bar the front entrance. That's where the TV cameras were. Our group of regulars went around to the back of the Center and sat down. Between us and the supply entrance stood a solid line of huge horses and their solemn police riders. We sat cross-legged, speaking softly as the day brightened. Sometimes someone would joke and someone else would immediately say, "Be serious." Off to one side, a captain watched us and the cavalry. Suddenly the horses reared, charged us as we sat, smashing us with their great bodies, scattering our supporting onlookers. People were knocked down, ran this way and that, but the horses were everywhere, rearing—until at the signal from the captain, which I saw, they stopped, settled down, and trotted away. That evening the papers and TV reported that a couple of thousand had demonstrated. Hundreds had been peacefully arrested.

At Wall Street too: A gentleman with a Wall Street attache case tried to get through our line. The police who were in the middle of a discussion about Arabian oil said, "Why not try down there, mister. You can get through down there." The gentleman said he wanted to get through right here and right now and began to knee through our line. The cop on the other side of the sawhorse said, "You heard us. Down there, mister. How about it?" The gentleman said, "Dammit, what are you here for?" He began to move away, calling back in fury, "What the hell are you cops here for anyway?" "Just role playing," the cop called in reply.

There were several cheerful police at the Trident demonstration last year. One officer cheerily called out to the Trident holiday visitors to be careful as they trod the heads of the demonstrators blocking the roadway. "They're doing what they believe in." He asked us to step back, but not more than six inches. He told a joke. He said he hated war, always had. Some young state troopers arrived—more help was needed. They were tall and grouchy. A Black youngster, about twelve, anxious to see what was going on, pushed against the line. One of the state troopers leaned forward and smacked the child hard on the side of the head. "Get back, you little bastard," he said. I reached out to get the attention of the cheery cop, who wore a piece of hierarchical gold on his jacket. "Officer," I said, "you ought to get that trooper out of here, he's dangerous." He looked at me, his face went icy cold, "Lady, be careful," he said. "I just saw you try to strike that officer."

Not too long ago, I saw Finnegan, the plainclothes Red Squad boss. I hadn't seen him in a long time. "Say, Finnegan," I said, "all these years you've been working at one thing and I've been working at the opposite, but look at us. Nothing's prevented either of us from getting gray." He almost answered, but a lot of speedy computations occurred in his brain, and he couldn't. It's the business of the armed forces and the armored face to maintain distance at all times.

On the Ramblas
A Tree   A Girl

Anyone would love to paint from memory
the bark of a plane tree in Barcelona
little geographies of burgundy turn to olive
before your very eyes or peel to that yellow
that pale cream of all the apartment rooms
in the Bronx

Or write one proper grieving song for the girl
beautiful but burned in face and arm
smoke smeared into lifelong recognition
screaming in Catalan at the man who stands
before her   who supplicates   whose hands
brought together in supplication
beg   for what
       pimp   lover   father?

I say   father   because I'm old
and know how we beg the young to live
no matter what

Four flights below us, leaning on the stoop, were about a dozen people and around them devastation. Just a minute, I said. I had seen devastation on my way, running, gotten some of the pebbles of it in my running shoe and the dust of it in my eyes. I had thought with the indignant courtesy of a citizen, This is a disgrace of the City of New York which I love and am running through.

But now, from the commanding heights of home, I saw it clearly. The tenement in which Jack my old and present friend had come to gloomy manhood had been destroyed, first by fire, then by demolition (which is a swinging ball of steel that cracks bedrooms and kitchens.) Because of this work, we could see several blocks wide and a block and a half long. Crazy Eddy's house still stood, famous 1510 gutted, with black window frames, no glass, open laths. The stubbornness of the supporting beams! Some persons or families still lived on the lowest floors. In the lots between, a couple of old sofas lay on their fat faces, their springs sticking up into the air. Just as in wartime a half-dozen ailanthus trees had already found their first quarter inch of earth and begun a living attack on the dead yards. At night, I knew animals roamed the place, squalling and howling, furious New York dogs and street cats and mighty rats. You would think you were in Bear Mountain Park, the terror of venturing forth.

Someone ought to clean that up, I said.

Mrs. Luddy said, Who you got in mind? Mrs. Kennedy?—

Donald made a stern face. He said, That just what I gonna do when I get big. Gonna get the Sanitary Man in and show it to him. You see that, you clean it up right now! Then he stamped his feet and fierced his eyes.

Excerpted from "The Long Distance Runner" in *Enormous Changes at the Last Minute*, published by Farrar, Straus & Giroux, 1974.

Across the River

There was the pretty town. There was the beautiful farm full of orchards and fields. There was the big barn. It burned. Silo and all. Cattle horses   pigs   the chicken house   1/3 of the orchard.

Almost immediately, in order to raise money, the women of the community began to design a patchwork quilt. It would be patched with the old cotton dresses of their little girls and their grandma's stored remnants. Little by little it became the history of the beautiful farm with solid colored dates, polka dotted outhouses on backgrounds of flowering cattle, light green hills specked with golden dandelions. Raffles were sold at all the banks but the event itself was saved for Labor Day so that the summer people could contribute to the good work.

There was also the small well-endowed college nearby. On its handsome campus, silk screened posters appeared asking for contributions to help restore the big barn to the beautiful farm.

One day in early June the trash truck came up the hill to our house. There was a young trashman and an old trashman on the truck. The young trashman shyly worked at our spring cleanup mess. I said to the old trashman – wasn't it hot for May? –   – No rain either – he said. – Awful day right now – I said. – Desperate for rain – he said.

– There must be lots of fires – I said. Many – he said.

I asked – Do you know that big place across the river, burned up, people are collecting money for it?

– I do – he said. Terrible fire. Collecting money, that's good of the kids. He looked sideways at our wood pile for a couple of minutes. – Have you thought of this? he asked turning to me. – Now what if a poor man's place burned? Small barn, a couple of cows no insurance. Why who'd help him? Maybe a couple of fellows from the firehouse or the Legion'd help nail some old boards. Would there be a collection? Would those college boys be running from door to door? No they wouldn't. The poor farmer would have to begin again like always like when his last barn went probably when he was young and there was help. And if this farmer was old and his boys disgusted with farming why – the old trashman shrugged and heaved a great black plastic bag of last summers junk into the truck – why it'd be too bad for that poor fool of a farmer wouldn't it?

The Women's Prison: El Salvador
The Ballad of Visiting Day

In Ilopongo Prison
        a girl is sitting quietly
She has only one leg   she
        wears a pretty dress and

her hair is done in braids
        her mother sits beside her
wearing a black dress her brother
        whistles through two reeds

and watches the sad women
        In Ilopongo prison
a little prisoner calls out Maria
        come talk to the North Americans

This prisoner has been a woman
        only a short time   she
wears a black beret   she wears
        a sash   she is a commandante

she fought away from girlhood
        in the high mountains of her country
Come come and tell your story
        to the North American women

about your brother Jaime
        martyred while still
a schoolboy   the mother hears
        his name Jaime   Jaime called

out loud   with her hand she brushes
        the dress all full of flowers
that she brought her daughter with one leg
        she sighs   she sighs deeply
you would think her body was
        a drum of thumping air

I stood inside our garden
        where we planted beans
the beans were climbing high
        five men came and whispered

-oh we are Jaime's friends
        oh how we long to see him
we knew him in the hills
        the little bumpy hills

that stumbled into mountains
        he said he had a sister
just like a morning rose
        that's how we recognized you

Tell us Maria   rosy beauty
        where is your brother Jaime
he's our brother too
        our comrade

I don't know where he is
        Come now little sister
you must tell us we lack
        all happiness without him

(There were five men)   believe me
        the last time that I saw him
those were the days of rain
        You stupid girl   you're lying

You're lying   liar tell us   we'll burn
        your mother's house   we are
the Guard now tell us   then
        one man raised his rifle   why?
I cried out   why?   Lightning
        slapped the earth beside me

All round the prison floor
        the little babies crawled
the mother looked at them
        she smoothed her daughter's dress

(the dress so full of flowers)
        Thank Mary   blessed virgin
that we were spared such shame
        The little commandante

cried out no shame no shame
        she banged the table hard
no shame   these children are not
        the first whose fathers are unknown

We are the babes of rape
        said the little commandante
our villages were torn our mothers
        violated   our fathers split in two

Still we have named our struggle
        for Farabundo Marti and we are
fierce and restless till justice and
        the land belong to the poor people

In Ilopongo Prison
        a girl is sitting quietly
she has only one leg   her mother
        sits beside her brushing
her long hair   her brother
        watches   whistles through two reeds
The little commandante talks
        with the North American women
the babies crying crawl toward
        the breasts of their lonesome mothers

The Dance in Jinoteca

In Jinoteca women greeted us
with thousands of flowers   roses
it was hard to tell   the petals
on our faces and arms   falling

Then embraces and the Spanish language
which is a little like a descent of
petals   pink   and orange

Suddenly out of the hallway   our
gathering place   AMNLAE   the
Associacion de Mujeres women
came running   seat yourselves dear
guests from the north   we   announce
a play   a dance   a play   the women
their faces mountain   river Indian
European   Spanish   dark haired
women

        dance   in grey green
fatigues   they dance the Contra who
circles the village waiting
for the young teacher   the health worker
(these are the strategies)   the farmer
in the high village walks out into the
morning toward the front which is a
circle of terror

            they dance
the work of women and men   they dance
the plowing of the field   they kneel
to the harrowing with the machetes   they
dance the sowing of seed (which is always
a dance) and the ripening of corn   the
flowers of grain   they dance the harvest
they raise their machetes for
the harvest   the machetes are high
                but no!

out of the hallway in green and grey
come those who dance the stealth
of the Contra   cruelly they
dance the ambush   the slaughter of
the farmer   they are the death dancers
who found the school teacher   they caught
the boy who dancing   brought seeds in
his hat all the way from Matagalpa they
dance the death of the mother the
father   the rape of the daughter   they
dance the child murdered the seeds
spilled and trampled   they dance
sorrow   sorrow

                    they dance the
search for the Contra   and the defeat
they dance a comic dance   they make a
joke of the puppetry of the Contra of
Uncle Sam who is the handler of puppets
they dance rage and revenge   they place
the dead child (the real sleeping baby)
on two chairs   which is the bier for
the little actor they dance prayer
bereavement   sorrow   they mourn

Is there applause for such theater?

Silence   then   come let us dance
together now you know   the usual
dance of couples Spanish or North
American   let us dance in two and
threes   let us make little circles let us
dance as though at a festival or in peace
time together and alone   whirling   stamping
our feet   bowing to one another

                   the children
gather petals from the floor to throw
at our knees   we dance   the children
too banging into us   into each other and
one small boy dances alone pulling
at our skirts   wait he screams stop!
he tugs at the strap of our camera   stop!
Stop dancing   I'm Carlos   take a picture
of me No!   Now!   Right now! because
soon   Look!   See Pepe!   even tomorrow
I could be dead like him

                   the music
catches its breath   the music
jumping in the guitar and phonograph holds
still and waits   no no we say Carlos
not you   we put our fingers on his little
shoulder we touch his hair but one of
us is afraid   for god's sakes take his
picture   so we lift him up   we photo-
graph him   we pass him from one to
another   we photograph him again and
again   with each of us   crying or
laughing with him in our arms
we dance

Answers I

What would that man think whose true propertarian wrath unhinged him the day after his own son tried publicly to set fire to the robes of Sister Veronica, driving him to seize and nearly strangle a certain eleven year old public school boy who had been leaning disrespectfully on his white Cadillac, mocking it before the other children so wholeheartedly that the man began to bang the boy's head on the railing of my building calling him brat and cuntsucker and other unheard of (by me) names right under my window, thereby involving the precinct police; what would he say if he knew that now, twenty years later the boy was solidly dead murdered in the wild mortal flower of young manhood on a distant highway by another auto-mobile probably of foreign make?

What would he say?

If sad rumor has it, he would reply: Oh but my son too, my son — not dead — but worse far worse.

Answers II

A man came into my father's workplace about eighty years ago. He held a gun and asked my father to hand over the shop's money. He was my father's brother. My father said "Why don't you ask me at home?" He answered, "Because I want your boss' money not the family's."

My father was 21 or 22, my uncle about 19. My father told me this story once. Most family stories are told many times.

One day my cousin Lenny and I were talking about the family. I wondered if he knew more about our uncle who had been taken from home, arrested in the Palmer Red raids of the early 20's and deported within the year to Russia, probably Vladivostok.

My cousin's mother, my aunt, the oldest sister took me aside and asked, "Why did you tell him this story? You don't even know what really happened. Let me tell you something. He was a wonderful boy our Grisha. You're so crazy about your father; but if you had known Grisha, with your crazy ideas you would have loved him much more. He was the one you would have loved."

POW

The lieutenant wondered about his luck. The year was 1969. He was a POW released into the custody of the peace movement in mid war.

"I don't know what I'll do," he said, "when I get back to the states."

"Well, you'll be glad to see your family, won't you?"

"Yes, naturally, but what'll I do to make a living?"

"Well, Jackson you know how to fly a plane. I bet there'll be plenty of jobs for pilots. You won't have any trouble."

"I don't want to do that."

"And the pay is probably damn good."

"No, no you don't get it. Flying back and forth—loading people then dumping them and picking up the next batch and flying back. It'd be like being a truck driver for some freight company."

"But you like flying, you said that."

"Yes." He looked out the window of the plane as far out and down as he could. "I love flying. But to be truthful, I have to say that I really liked bombing. I don't know why I liked it."

The other POW who'd been released, the Captain, leaned over our seats. In 1967, this Captain had been trying his best to destroy the great Thanh Hoa bridge. He had hoped he'd get a chance to see the damage when the Vietnamese took the pilots—for purposes of conscience building—to see what was left of the villages they'd bombed.

"I knew they wouldn't fly us over Thanh Hoa," he said. "Listen Jackson, we're coming into Bangkok. I hope they debrief me there. Anyway," he said, "when we get there remember if they ask us anything, I'll do the talking. I'm the senior man here. You sometimes forget. Keep it in mind."

"Sure enough sir," said Jackson, "You are the senior officer, you do the talking, it's up to you sir."

"How can you speak to him like that?" I muttered. "He's such a creep."

"That's another thing you don't understand," Jackson said.

"It's the airforce. It's the marines. It's the army. Don't you get it? It's the way the world is."

"No it isn't, '" I said.

Three Days and a Question

On the first day I joined a demonstration opposing the arrest in Israel of members of Yesh Gvul, Israeli soldiers who had refused to serve in the occupied territories. Yesh Gvul means: *There is a Limit.*

TV cameras and an anchorwoman arrived and *New York Times* stringers with their narrow journalism notebooks. What do you think? the anchorwoman asked. What do you think, she asked a woman passer-by—a woman about my age.

Anti-Semites, the woman said quietly.

The anchorwoman said, But they're Jewish.

Anti-Semites, the woman said, a little louder.

What? One of our demonstrators stepped up to her. Are you crazy? How can you...Listen what we're saying.

Rotten anti-Semites—all of you.

What? What What the man shouted. How you dare to say that —all of us Jews. Me, he said. He pulled up his shirtsleeve. Me? You call me? You look. He held out his arm. Look at this.

I'm not looking, she screamed.

You look at my number, what they did to me. My arm...you have no right.

Anti-Semite, she said between her teeth. Israel hater.

No, no he said, you fool. My arm—you're afraid to look...my arm...my arm.

On the second day Vera and I listen at PEN to Eta Krisaeva read her stories that were not permitted publication in her own country, Czechoslovakia. Then we walk home in the New York walking night, about twenty blocks—shops and lights, other walkers talking past us. Late-night homeless men and women asleep in dark storefront doorways on cardboard pallets under coats and newspapers, scraps of blanket. Near home on Sixth Avenue a young man, a boy, passes—a boy the age a younger son could be—head down, bundles in his arms, on his back.

Wait, he says, turning to stop us. Please, please wait. I just got out of Bellevue. I was sick. They gave me something. I don't know...I need to sleep somewhere. The Y, maybe.

That's way uptown.

Yes, he says. He looks at us. Carefully he says, AIDS. He looks away. Oh. Separately, Vera and I think: A boy—only a boy. Mothers after all, our common trade for more than thirty years.

Then he says, I put out my hand. We think he means to tell us he tried to beg. I put out my hand. No one will help me. No one.

Because they can see. Look at my arm. He pulls his coatsleeve back. Lesions, he says. Have you ever seen lesions? That's what people see.

No. No, we see a broad fair forehead, a pale countenance, fear. I just have to sleep, he says.

We shift in our pockets. We give him what we find—about eight dollars. We tell him, Son, they'll help you on 13th Street at the Center. Yes, I know about that place. I know about them all. He hoists the bundle of his things to his back to prepare for walking. Thank you, ladies. Goodbye.

On the third day I'm in a taxi. I'm leaving the city for a while and need to get to the airport. We talk—the driver and I. He's a black man, dark. He's not young. He has a French accent. Where are you from? Haiti, he answers. Ah, your country is in bad trouble. Very bad. You know that, Miss.

Well, yes. Sometimes it's in the paper.

They thieves there. You know that? Very rich, very poor. You believe me? Killing—it's nothing to them, killing. Hunger. Starving people. Everything bad. And you don't let us come. Starving. They send us back.

We're at a red light. He turns to look at me. Why they do that? He doesn't wait for me to say, Well…because…He says, Why hard.

The light changes. We move slowly up traffic-jammed Third Avenue. Silence. Then, Why? Why they let the Nicaragua people come? Why they let Vietnamese come? One time American people want to kill them people. Put bomb in their children. Break their head. Now they say, Yes Yes, come come come. Not us. Why?

Your New York is beautiful country. I love it. So beautiful, this New York. But why, tell me, he says, stopping the cab, switching the meter off. Why, he says, turning to me again, rolling his short shirtsleeve back, raising his arm to the passenger divider, pinching and pulling the bare skin of his upper arm. You tell me—this skin, this black skin—why? Why you hate this skin so much?

Question: Those gestures, those arms, the three consecutive days thrown like a formal net over the barest unchanged accidental facts. How? Why? In order to become—probably—in this city one story told.

In France

Poor talker   mouthperson
    alone
waiting for bravery

the muse (in
    other words)
      OH language

circumvent my tongue
    tell pen
      Move!

Make text

Autumn

What is sometimes called a
         tongue of flame
or an arm extended burning
         is only the long
red and orange branch of
         a green maple
in early September   reaching
         into the greenest field
out of the green woods   at the
         edge of which the birch trees
appear a little tattered   tired
         of sustaining delicacy
all through the hot summer re-
         minding everyone (in
our family)   of a Russian
         song   a story
by Chekov   or my father

For George

What was left   before crumbling
was sweetness in the maple leaf

in our friend George   a brilliant
attentive sweetness

in the wild red maple leaf
before winter   in our friend
George Dennison   before death

For Mike and Jeannie: Resisters
Fifteen Years Later

The car turned over three times
rolled down the nice
summertime hayfield

at the riverbank   the boy
hung upside down in his seat belt
glass   glittering dust
          in his hair   on his long lashes
          gently we brushed his bloodly lips
          Did I live?   he asked

Then Mike said   Look!   sometimes
          what you see   you see your own death

I want to know
who saw you Mike   with Jeannie
on that Virginia road   six months later
          tilting   tilting into the
          rain softened shoulder   over
          over   down   flung
from that tin can of a car

did one of you see the   other
dead   did one of you say
No   No   Us?

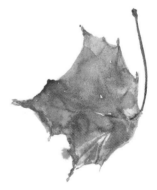

Conversation: Some History

"What the hell are we doing here?" asks an old friend, who was young in years not so long ago, when I was only slightly middle-aged. "For Christ's sake, we cut right through the fences at the Pentagon." We were in Seabrook, NH, sitting in a parking lot outside the site of a proposed nuclear plant along with 2,000 other protesters organized by the Clamshell Alliance.

"No! No!" says a young listener, full of the joy of common discipline.

"But look, it's a goddamn parking lot!"

"Things don't have to go the same," I say. I am very tearful. 'We don't have to defend our lives by repeating them. Anyhow, the parking lot is the heart of America. You close down the parking lots, and industry is wrecked. A decent car wouldn't have any place to go. Of course, those bubbling asphalt lots will be hard to occupy in summer."

The young listener says the simplest true fact. "Look, brother, it took a lot of work to get 2,000 people here. If we were only 200, we wouldn't have gotten to this lot. We'd be outside the access road at the Stop 'n Shop, eating cheeseburgers."

"Not me," said a young woman. "I would never eat that stuff." She is carrying a four-day supply of healthy groceries and offers us her family granola.

I have my own kitchen concoction of grains, fruits, and nuts. 'Yours is very good," I tell her, "but you use more nuts than I do. Try some of mine."

"How long are you staying here?"

"Well, no longer than Monday morning. We can't stay any longer," I apologize.

She puts her kind hand on mine. "Oh, don't feel bad. You've done your best. You can only do your best."

I know what my best is, and I have to admit to her that this is my second best. But, "How long are you staying, honey?"

"Oh," she says, "a week, anything, as long as I can."

"What if we're all arrested tomorrow morning?"

"Well, as soon as we get out, we'll return, we really will. Our affinity group is solidly committed to return."

Within the comfort of our affinity group, we place our sleeping bags on oak leaves over the sand and stone. We have named our street Karen Silkwood Drive and our new tent city is called Seabrook. It's quite beautiful—the American-Russian moon shines on the green, blue, yellow, orange plastic and nylon tents.

Late in the morning (9 a.m.) my husband goes off to listen to the almost continuous parliament of Spokespersons sent from each affinity group to bring views and initiatives to the Decision Making Body—the DMB. A new democratic process is being created.

"They never stop talking," someone says.

"Everyone has something to say," someone answers.

I decide to attend a Friends meeting on the northeast corner near the helicopter gate, the national guardsmen, and now and then the dogs. We sit on the stony landfill, the dust blowing. I say to myself, why this must be just what Quang Tri looked like— the bulldozed, flattened, "pacified" countryside. I can't help those connections. They stand up among the thoughts in my head, again and again.

Anyway, I'm not very good at Friends meetings. My mind refuses to prevent my eyes from looking at the folks around me, and I'm often annoyed because I can't get the drift of the murmur of private witness. I did hear one young man near me say, "May Your intercession here today be the fruit of our action." I think this means, "God helps those that help themselves," a proverb that sounds meaner than it is.

Finally a woman as gray as I am spoke up loud and clear. She intended to be heard. She told about the Westover Army Base witness during the Vietnam War. She had met a soldier later, she said, who told her it was the persistence and sagacity of the Quaker witness at Westover that had helped those draftees understand the war and turn in action against it.

The arrests begin at 3:30 and continue for 13 hours. People are moved in buses and trucks. There is lots of time for argument— no, discussion—to go limp, to go rigid. In the end, many give up the luxury of individual torture for the security of arrest by affinity. So we are picked up and dumped into an army truck at 7:30. Twenty-seven of us remain sitting or organized into sardines, we sleep on the floor until morning. One of our clan stands talking to the state troopers and guardsmen, some of whom haven't slept for 46 hours. He talks and listens all night long, about the war, about Phu Bai, where he was stationed, about the navy, the marines, horses, actions, guard duty, guns. A man's life, I think. I had forgotten the old interests and disgusts.

In the morning, Steve, the Clamshell staff man, who is 20 years old, types out our first news release. He tapes it to a frisbee, and David, his brother Clam, with a great swing, flips it out over the Army snowfence into the hands of the UPI photographer. The national guardsmen watch, then bring us cokes and orange soda.

I write this on the sixth day. Fourteen hundred people have remained in bail solidarity inside the detention centers of New Hampshire. There is no peaceful atom, and in our time war has been declared across the years against the future, which was once the holding place for hope.

One more story.

In another time, my friend and I vigiled every Saturday afternoon for eight years on Eighth Street in Manhattan. We offered information and support for resistance to war—legal and illegal, civilian and military. We were mostly mothers and fathers. The faces on our posters were American and Vietnamese. On our square in the middle of traffic, we were attacked for years with spit, curses, and scary driving tactics. Then, in the last two years, to our surprise, people began to shout, "Right on! Stick with it!"

One day, an old lady stopped me as I was giving out leaflets. I loved her at once, because she reminded me of my own mother and several aunts, who seemed in their construction to have only good posture to offer in the fight against gravity.

"They're wonderful boys," she said.

"Oh, yes," I said.

"We have to do everything we can for them," she said.

"We do," I said.

"Because what's going on, what they're trying to do to them, is terrible, especially to the Vietnamese people, how they suffer, without end," she said.

"Yes," I said.

"So you have to keep it up, the support. The boys sit in jail, I know what it's like. They don't want to kill people, they give up everything, they're brave, they're the hope."

I remembered my job. "Can you join us? To stand with our big sign over there, or give out leaflets in case you hate to stand?"

"No, no, I can't do it right now. Sometime maybe."

"Could you give me your name? We're a local group."

"Yes, certainly," she said. "My name is Sobell, I'm Morton Sobell's mother."

I said, "Oh, Morton Sobell. Oh...."

Then, without a thought, we fell into each others' arms and began to cry, because her son was still at that time hopelessly in jail and had been there for years, all through his young manhood. And the sons and daughters of my friends were caught in a time of war that would use them painfully, no matter what their decisions.

Then we were embarrassed. We kissed each other, we nodded, we laughed at ourselves, we said "Enough!" She crossed the street, and I continued to give out leaflets.

PEOPLE IN MY FAMILY

In my family
people who are 82 are very different
from people who are 92

The 82-year old people grew up
The year was 1914
This is what they knew   World War I
War   World War   War
That's why when they speak to the grandchild
they say   poor little one

The 92-year old people grew up
The year was 1905
          They went to prison
          They went into exile
          They said ah   soon
That's why when they speak to the grandchild
they say   first there will be revolution
then there will be revolution   then once more
then   the earth itself will turn and turn
and cry out   Oh I have been made sick
          then you   my little bud
          will flower and save it.

Conversations

Faith had just returned from Puerto Rico. She had attended a conference on The Bilingual Child and Public Education. She was an active worker in the PTA and had been sent by the local school board.

The neighborhood newspaper, always longing for community news, wanted to interview her. The young reporter made a couple of remarks, then asked a general question. "Mrs. Asbury, I understand you talked with many people and visited schools and clinics as part of the work of this conference. What did you think of Puerto Rico?"

Luckily she had been forming and reforming some sentences on the plane. She was able to deliver them—awkward but whole. "I think: first, around 1900 we stole their language from the people. The U.S. commissioners decided the Puerto Ricans should be educated in English—just the way the French did with the Vietnamese. Then, around the time the schools and the children were freed finally into their native Spanish, our cities needed new cheap labor, and the people were stolen from their language. That's what I think."

"May I quote you?" he asked.

"Yes," said Faith, feeling like the great traveler. "Quote me."

In the evening, she persuaded her son Richard to accompany her. They visited her parents, who lived in the Home for the Golden Ages, an institution full of small apartments for the intact, and dormitories for those unable to care for themselves. She told her parents that she had been interviewed and would soon be quoted. Her mother went next door immediately to inform a neighbor.

"I hope you didn't make a fool of yourself," her father said nervously.

"She handles herself pretty well lately," said Richard. "Don't worry Grandpa. I worry sometimes myself," he said courteously. His grandfather looked at him and nearly fainted with love. "He looks wonderful, this boy," he said. "I like his hair long."

"I do too," said Faith's mother, returning with her friend Mrs. Harrison. "I told her you would be in the paper. She wanted to meet you."

"Oh Ma, it's just a little neighborhood paper."

"All right, my dream," her mother said. "You took a trip. You went to a different place. Tell us something."

"Well, okay." said Faith. "First, it's very beautiful. Very green and mountainous and you know, an island. They call it Daughter of the Sun and Sea. They can grow anything—oranges, bananas, beans, tomatoes, avocados—anything—people have chickens—but you know I went into a supermarket and *the eggs are all stamped U.S.A.!*"

Mrs. Harrison said, "They're poor people, I suppose. We send them eggs? It's wonderful. That's the good old U.S. of A. for you."

"Wonderful...." said Richard. "Wonderful? Don't you people understand anything?"

"What a temper!" said his grandfather, full of admiration. "What Richard means Mrs. Harrison: We don't *give* them. We *sell* them. They *got* to buy the eggs. They quit doing all that agriculture themselves."

"Sure, we even send them rice from California," said Faith, "—which they could also grow."

"They should do it if they can," said Mrs. Harrison. "But the tropics....people get very lackadaisical, I suppose."

"You suppose," said Richard. He stood up and looked at the door.

"Calm down," said Faith. "Let me explain it a little. You know, when I visited one of the junior highs, I went into the kitchen—first of all I must say the school was beautiful—on a hill, a campus really. In the kitchen, I met these women very familiar to me, Puerto Rican women, after all, I know them from the PTA. And it turned out that a few, more than a few, had been in the States, worked in New York, it was too hard. On Rivington Street as a matter of fact...."

"You're supposed to be explaining something," said Richard.

"I don't happen to have your machine-gun style, Richard, so just shut up! Where was I? The women. The women were school kitchen aides and they had these enormous bags of rice from California on the table and they were taking all sorts of little bugs and worms out of the rice."

"You see," said Richard, who couldn't be quiet another minute, "you see they not only squeeze the local people out with cheap U.S.A. prices but they send them junk. They do that all over. That's what it means to be a colony, you get junk. You're poor. You gotta take it. Junky rice, inflammable clothes, you *could* grow oranges but can't afford it. It comes cheaper from three thousand miles away even including the oil. You want to know a fact. Little Puerto Rico was our fifth biggest market. A fact."

"He's right," said Faith, "it's not such a surprising idea—it happens right here. People are poor but they think they're rich. They own a houseful of plastic and tin."

"And who needs it?" asked Mrs. Harrison, who still refused to argue. "Garbage! But the president just said they could become a state."

"A state! What's so great about becoming a state? They already have the honor of having more dead and wounded guys from the last war, percentagewise. And look at Maine—they're giving all the shoe business to Korea. Maine's a colony, Vermont's a colony. A state! Big deal. Thank you U.S.A."

"He does have a wonderful temper," said Mrs. Harrison.

"*He* was once like that," said his grandmother, poking her husband in the ribs.

"And what about you? Once upon a time, *I* remember," he said smiling. "Once, on the boardwalk, she socked a cop who grabbed our boy for some foolishness."

This finished everything for Richard. "He was *once* like that. You were *once*. No wonder the world's in this condition. *Once!*" he shouted, and tore out of the apartment as though "*Once*" were catching, a contagious disease which might afflict his revolutionary limbs forever, and set the muscles of his face in an ineradicable smile.

Life in the Country
A City Friend Asks "Is it Boring?"

No! Living in the country is extremely lively, busy. After the gardens have gone to flower, to seed, to frost, the fruits canned, frozen, dried, the days and evenings are full of social event and human communication. Most of it dependent on the automobile or phone, though a few tasks can be accomplished on foot or ski.

Even if you are not worried about the plain physical future of the world, there's a lot to do. If you are concerned about your village there are zoning meetings, water board meetings, school meetings and school board meetings, PTA meetings. There's the Improvement Society, whose main task is sustaining the life of the Green or Common as the elms die away from us. There's also the Ladies Benevolent whose name explains itself. For some there is the interesting Historical Society of their town; there are selectmen meetings. There's the conservation committee, the agricultural committee for those who count the farms each year and find several missing. There are the food COOP meetings one for ordering, one for distributing, one for the COOP board. For those who love theater, there are groups flourishing in several of the towns of the county, all requiring lots of rehearsal, costume making and in the event of a success, traveling to other towns. Of course many of these meetings happen in bad weather, ice, sleet, and require pot luck suppers, so there is a great deal of cooking and baking.

All of this liveliness happens after the workday world and the meetings of that world union or managerial. Nor have I mentioned purely social events, returning a neighbor's dinner invitation, going to a church supper, a fair, the high school basketball game, or square dance for the pleasure of it.

Many of us fearing the world's end, and saddened by our country's determined intervention, have been involved in political work and this requires the following: one meeting every two weeks of our affinity group, a meeting every month or two of a coalition, the special legal meetings which usually precede and follow illegal actions. Then the frequent meetings once an action has been decided upon. If these actions include civil disobedience there will be training meetings as well as legal ones, so that by role playing and other methods we retain our non-violent beliefs and strategies.

And then there is ordinary life. For instance, there is keeping the mud and hay out of the house and stacking the wood in the wood shed. There is also stuffing newspapers and rags into the cracks and chinks that each new descent of temperature exposes. There is also skiing across shining fields and through dangerous woods full of trees one must avoid.

And of course there is standing in the front yard (or back) staring at the work time has accomplished in crumpling the hills into mountains then stretching them out again only a few miles away into broad river plains, stippling white pink rust black across the wooded hills, clarifying the topography by first aging, then blowing away the brilliant autumn leaves. Although here and there, the wrinkled brown leaves of the oak hold tight and the beech leaf whose tree will die young, grows daily more transparent but waits all winter for the buds of spring.

Fear

I am afraid of nature
because of nature   I am mortal

my children and my grandchildren
are also mortal

I lived in the city for forty years
in this way   I escaped fear

Two Old Stories

The first story: A woman is pregnant. One morning she wakes up in a pool of blood. Miscarriage. She calls her doctor. (It's thirty years ago.) "So," he says "What did you do?" She thinks he's joking. "Shall I come over to the office?" "No!" he says. "Try to get help. Don't come."

She continues to bleed. She thinks. She doesn't think. Finally, three days later she calls again. After all, he's her doctor. He says glumly, "OK, come." She asks him, "What's going on?" "It's hard," he answers. Another doctor friend explains. "He's probably being watched he thinks. He's a good guy. He may have helped someone. He's afraid."

The second story: A woman is bleeding. This is not unusual, but the bleeding continues for days. Ten days, then eleven. She becomes weak. She's a small slim woman. Daily, frightening amounts of blood leave her.

She hasn't been working and is worried about money. She goes to the emergency room of her neighborhood hospital. There they say they cannot really examine her. Suppose she's pregnant. The foetus might be disturbed. (It's a Catholic Hospital.) She will have to wait for the rabbit test—a couple of days. (It's thirty years ago.) She begins to bleed fearfully. Hemorrhage. Luckily the test returns. She is not pregnant. They are able now, morally, to examine her. She has a large tumor and must be operated on immediately.

I tell these stories whenever I can. Why? Partly because they happened frequently to women before Roe v. Wade and can't have legally happened since that decision. Also they're not about abortion. Mostly I tell the stories to show, in the experience of my generation, the way in which the passion for the fetus is only the tip of the iceberg of male power and concern. That deep proprietary interest is in the womb, the cervix, the belly, the vagina, the entire female body, which once it's stolen from us will end probably for decades all our new, free womanly rights to those good companions sex and love.

Bridges

Along the beach beyond La Boca   the Luquillo River
stretches and bends to reach the sea   in tropical
easiness it takes no trouble   at high tide the ad-
venturous sea pours salt into the eyes of the
sweet water fish

Clouds blow and darken toward the mists of the
rain forest mountain   sun falls from the aging
day and looks at night   but first it shines the
palm leaves blinding the lizards

Fifty feet toward sunset the river widens   it was
once two rivers   I can see the far glint of a steel
bridge   cars moving fast on Route Three

A dark form stands in the Luquillo River   an old bridge
pillar and planks rotted   unconnected to either shore

Long ago in morning shadow this bridge rattled the
campesinos and the pescadores in their carts hurrying
to Fajardo   they travelled in sight of the fishy
noisy sea

There were four bridges over the river near Nien Trach
south south of Tonkin Bay north of Quangh Binh   three
were splintered and burned   torn from their village
shores   one stood   a dyke of mud and rocks as wide
as a small truck

We drive to the airport near San Juan   the sea on one hand
the darkening river the old unconnected bridge   a platform
on mossy stilts   the traffic is heavy on Route Three
called by American Army Engineers   The Road of the
Sixty-fifth Infantry

In the Bus

Somewhere between Greenfield and Holyoke
snow became rain
and a child passed through me
As a person moves through mist
as the moon moves through
a dense cloud at night
as though I were cloud or mist
a child passed through me

On the highway that lies
across miles of stubble
and tobacco barns our bus speeding
speeding disordered the slanty rain
and a girl with no name naked
wearing the last nakedness of
childhood breathed in me
                    once no
                    two breaths
a sigh   she whispered   Hey you
begin again
              Again?
again   again   you'll see
it's easy   begin again   long ago

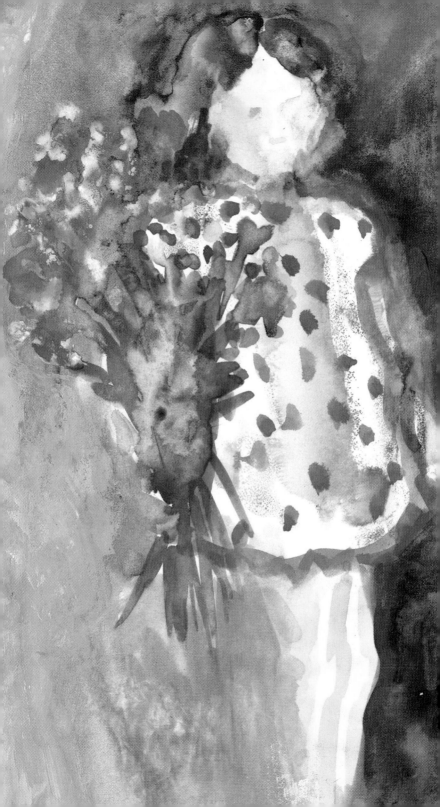

The Feminist Press at The City University of New York
311 East 94 Street
New York, NY 10128

The Feminist Press at The City University of New York offers
alternatives in education and in literature. Founded in 1970,
this nonprofit, tax-exempt educational and publishing organiza-
tion works to eliminate sexual stereotypes in books and schools
and to provide literature with a broad vision of human potential.

New Society Publishers/East   New Society Publishers/West
5427 Springfield Avenue   P.O. Box 582
Philadelphia, PA 19143   Santa Cruz, CA 95061

New Society Publishers is a worker-controlled, nonprofit pub-
lishing house committed to fundamental social change through
nonviolent action. New Society Publishers is a project of the
New Society Educational Foundation, a nonprofit, tax-exempt
public foundation.

War Resisters League
National Office
339 Lafayette Street
New York, NY 10012

War Resisters League was organized in 1923 by women and men
who had opposed the First World War. WRL is committed to
eliminating not only war, but the causes of war. WRL advocates
the theory and practice of nonviolence as the method for creat-
ing a democratic society free of war, racism, sexism, and human
exploitation.